SERAPIS, an Egyptian deity who became the Greek god of Alexandria. Eastern religions were introduced into Roman Britain, their devotees belonging mainly to the Roman army. This fine head, bearing a "modius", or corn measure, was found on the site of the temple of Mithras discovered in the City of London in 1954.

Frontispiece

JOURNEYS THROUGH
OUR EARLY HISTORY

THE
ROMAN
EPOCH IN
BRITAIN

by
Colin Clair

BRUCE & GAWTHORN LTD.
Hunters Lane, Leavesden, Watford, Herts.

Introduction

THIS England was once, and remained for nearly four centuries, a province of the great Roman Empire.

The immediate permanent effects of Roman rule, after the withdrawal of the occupying power, seem on the face of it to have been slight. In England Latin never took the place of the language of the conquered people as it did in Spain and Gaul. Though the magnificent Roman roads remained, the towns were laid waste and left to crumble into ruins and there is no evidence that any Roman town was continuously occupied after the invasions of the Anglo-Saxons.

Of the 300 years after the departure of the Romans we know little; these are the so-called "Dark Ages." Dimly we can make out a land harassed by war and devastated by invaders. A troubled time, in which much of the civilizing influence of the Roman colonizers was undone. Yet the influence of that occupation did in some ways remain. Neither Jutes, Angles nor Saxons destroyed the Romano-British population, nor did they entirely extinguish the embers kindled from the Roman fire.

The many improvements in domestic and social life introduced during the Roman occupation lingered on after their departure and the influence of the government of Rome survived not only in laws and customs, which withstood the English Conquest, but also in husbandry, for the Romans had turned the Britons from a purely pastoral into an agricultural community.

Moreover, Christianity, introduced into the land in the time of the Romans, remained the religion of those parts which escaped the English Conquest and was later to play a great part in the cultural development of the Anglian kingdom of Northumbria.*

Of late, as a result of the work of historians and archaeologists, considerable interest has been aroused concerning that early period in our history. This little book is intended as a simple introduction to the Roman epoch in Britain.

* See Northumbria, a companion volume in this series.

THE ROMAN EPOCH IN BRITAIN

THE COMING OF THE ROMANS

ON August 26th, 55 B.C., watchers on the English cliffs near Dover saw Roman war galleys riding at anchor in the Channel. In one of them was the Roman commander in Gaul, the Consul Gaius Julius Caesar. With him were the 7th and 10th Legions with archers and slingers, a force of nearly ten thousand men.

The arrival of this force was not unexpected. During his campaigns in Gaul Caesar had come into contact with Commius, King of the Atrabates, a tribe which lived on both sides of the Channel, having spread from their original home in the north of France to the south of England, around Hampshire and Berkshire. Commius knew from experience the might of Roman arms, and at Caesar's suggestion he sought to persuade rulers of other British tribes that it would be useless to resist the power of Rome, and that they would do better to acknowledge Roman suzerainty straight away.

But one ruler would have none of this: he was Cassivellaunus, King of the Catuvellauni, a powerful chief

ROMAN BRITAIN

who ruled in Hertfordshire and had his capital at Verulam (St. Albans). He scorned the idea and imprisoned Commius. Of this, Caesar, who looked for an unopposed landing, was not aware.

The galleys remained motionless, for Caesar was awaiting the transports containing his cavalry, which had missed the tide. At last, when the tide was on the turn, Caesar would wait no longer and sailed up the Channel in search of a likely landing place.

A little later, at Walmer, on the Kentish coast, the standard-bearer of the 10th Legion jumped into the surf, calling upon his comrades to follow. A force of Britons, which had marched along the cliffs keeping the Romans in view, attempted to oppose the landing, but the disciplined veterans of the campaigns in Gaul soon put the Britons to flight.

Unfortunately for Caesar, however, he had no cavalry with which to pursue them; no horsemen to spy out the strength and position of the opposing forces. It was an army without eyes. It could not, as yet, venture inland.

THEN a serious disaster overtook the invaders. A fierce gale in the Channel again beat back the cavalry transports to the French coast and, at the same time, wrecked most of the galleys and transports which were lying off Walmer. While the Romans were feverishly trying to make their vessels seaworthy once more, the British chiefs had gathered reinforcements and suddenly swept down upon the legionaries, who were isolated on a hostile shore with no reserves of men or supplies to call upon.

But Caesar's own bravery and skill in leading his small force, allied to the military experience of his soldiers, not only averted disaster, but once more defeated the British. Whereupon Caesar deemed it wise to return to France. On

GAIUS JULIUS CAESAR

Gaius Julius Caesar was born about the year 102 B.C., and first distinguished himself as a soldier at the siege of Mitylene during the second Mithridatic War. From 58 to 49 B.C. he was proconsul in Gaul and in Illyricum (on the Adriatic sea opposite Italy) conducting the campaigns described in his *Commentaries*. The highlight of his career was his defeat of Pompey during the first Civil War, which made him master of Rome. He was assassinated on the March 15th, 44 B.C., by a band of conspirators headed by Marcus Brutus and Gaius Cassius. From a marble bust in the Palazzo dei Conservatori, Campidoglio.

ROMAN BRITAIN

the whole, the expedition had been something of a fiasco.

A second attempt was better organized. As soon as he returned to France Caesar arranged for the building of a fleet of 600 transports and 28 war galleys as well as for the collection of vast stores. The following summer, in the month of July, he embarked with five Legions and 2,000 cavalry, leaving another large force near Boulogne as a reserve and to protect his base from any Gallic attack during his absence.

This time the landing, which was made in the vicinity of Sandwich, was unopposed. The Britons, alarmed at the vast number of vessels, took refuge inland, waiting to attack (as Caesar himself has related) until the Roman force came to a river on its march inland.

Disaster again almost overtook the Romans at the

Below, part of the interior of the Roman fort at Richborough in Kent. In the area enclosed by the buildings in the foreground were found many pigs of lead, which suggests that this portion was the Roman foundry. *Rutupial*, as the Romans called it, became the chief disembarkation port for legionaries from the Continent. (*See* also page 57.)

Site of a gateway at the old Roman camp at Richborough. From this gate issued the road known as Watling Street. Part of the paving of the gateway is visible in the foreground. Watling Street ran through Canterbury, and went then, by way of London, Fenny Stratford and Towcester, to Chester, which was a Roman fortress.

outset. After they had defeated a British force near Canterbury, news came that another terrific gale had wrecked 40 of their transports and damaged many more. At once Caesar marched his army back to the coast where, for more than ten days and nights, protected by hastily dug earthworks, they toiled to repair the damage.

They then resumed their march; but while they had been thus delayed the tribes of the Belgae, who lived in the south of Britain, in Hampshire and Wiltshire, united under the leadership of Cassivellaunus to oppose the invaders.

However, the Britons, though brave and resolute, were no match for the skilled, and, above all, disciplined Roman army, and although they harassed Caesar's troops from time to time as he advanced, he soon reached and captured the capital of Cassivellaunus, though the king himself had fled.

Thereupon the tribes yielded and Caesar, through the intermediary of Commius, whom he had released, received the submission of Cassivellaunus and other British kings. Nevertheless, once again Caesar's visit to these shores was destined to be a short one. News reached him of an impending revolt in Gaul and he withdrew his army from Britain and returned to France to cope with this menace. He had been in Britain less than two months.

★ ★ ★ ★ ★

THE SECOND INVASION

ALMOST a hundred years elapsed before the Romans returned. Nevertheless, the Romanization of Britain had begun, fostered by the development of trade between this island and Roman Gaul. The permanent conquest and subjugation of the island was not accomplished until the great invasion of A.D. 43, in the reign of the Roman Emperor Claudius.

Why, after leaving Britain alone for nearly a century, did the Romans suddenly decide to conquer and occupy Britain? There were probably several reasons. One is given by the ancient geographer, Strabo, who, describing the chief countries in the Roman world, said: "Britain produces corn and fodder and gold and silver and iron. These are imported by us, as well as hides and slaves and good hunting hounds." Certainly the reputed wealth of Britain was a most likely reason, and the Roman official and historian, Tacitus, son-in-law of Agricola, who was a distinguished governor of Britain, has stated that the

THE SECOND LANDING

Romans hoped to find great wealth in the British mines.

Other reasons were possibly the desire of the Emperor Claudius to begin his reign (he had succeeded Caligula in A.D. 41) with some spectacular feat of arms; the prevailing disunity in Britain, where the older-established tribes were at loggerheads with the more recently arrived and warlike Belgic tribes; and finally, perhaps, a geographical misconception.

The Romans imagined that Spain lay much farther to the north-west than it does, and that Ireland lay midway between it and Britain. Tacitus considered that the conquest and occupation of Ireland would be a useful step in Roman colonial expansion, for, he said: "Ireland, since it lies midway between Britain and Spain and is easily reached from the Gaulish Sea would have linked the strongest part of the empire [Britain, Gaul and Spain] together to the mutual advantage of them all."

THE expeditionary force, under the command of Aulus Plautus, consisted of some five Roman legions* together with a large body of auxiliary troops, both horse and foot, the total number being over 40,000. Little is known of the actual circumstances of the landing, for the only account which has come down to us is that by Dio Cassius, a Roman governor of Africa, who wrote a voluminous Roman History; but his account was written some 150 years after the event. It seems probable that the main landing was made at Richborough, in Kent, though some authorities favour the vicinity of Hayling Island, in Hampshire.

Accounts differ, also, as to whether the landing was, or was not opposed, but it seems clear that Aulus Plautus met serious resistance only at one point, when they came to "the passage of a river," as Dio Cassius puts it, without

---
* *The 2nd, 9th, 14th and 20th legions together with a large part of the 8th.*

ROMAN BRITAIN

informing us whether this was, as some think, the Thames, or, as others conjecture, the Medway. Wherever it was, strong resistance was made by the sons of Cunobeline (the Cymbeline of Shakespeare's play), Togodumnus and Caractacus (Caradoc), during which battle the former was killed.

After that the Romans met with little serious opposition and soon reached and captured Camulodonum, the royal city of Cunobeline, on the site of which has grown up the present Colchester. Meanwhile, the Emperor Claudius himself had arrived in Britain and made a state entry into Camulodonum, accompanied by a procession of elephants, a strange sight surely for those ancient Britons. There can have been little fighting at this time, for Claudius only stayed in Britain for 16 days, during which time, according to an inscription in the Palazzo Barbarini in Rome, he received the submission of 11 British kings. Afterwards he returned to Rome, where he held a great Triumph and gave his infant son the name of Britannicus.

DURING the next seven years the Romans consolidated their position, moving steadily westward and northward. Before A.D. 49 the lead mines on the Mendips were being exploited, and several military roads had been built. The 2nd legion was stationed at Gloucester and the 9th at Lincoln.

The main threat to the Romans now came from the hills of Wales and the Pennines. In Wales the fugitive Caractacus was stirring up discontent among the Silures, a fierce tribe who were unwilling to submit to Roman domination, while in the hills and on the moors of the northern counties the powerful tribe of the Brigantes, ill-controlled by their Queen Cartismandua, gave a certain amount of trouble.

Caractacus held out for a time in the mountains of North Wales but was finally defeated by Ostorius Scapula, who had succeeded Aulus Plautus as governor. He was taken

MASSACRE OF THE DRUIDS

Above, the site of one of the old Roman lead workings at Chaterhouse in the Mendips. Lead mines were worked extensively by the Romans in many parts of Britain, but the greatest output was from the mines on the Mendip Hills. The ground is still pitted with small hollows called "buddles" at places where the mining was carried on.

prisoner and sent to Rome, where presumably he spent the remainder of his life.

But the Silures continued to give trouble and when Suetonius Paulinus became governor, in A.D. 51, he determined to crush them once and for all. His army reached the island of Anglesey in the year A.D. 61 in a campaign during which there was a great massacre of the Druids, accompanied by the destruction of their shrines.

While this campaign was in progress, however, Suetonius learned of a new danger. Infuriated by the malpractices of local officials and embittered by the confiscation of some of their land as grants to time-expired legionaries as well as by the taxes imposed for the maintenance of the Temple of Claudius at Camulodonum, the tribe of the Iceni, in

ROMAN BRITAIN

An arch-druid in his judicial robes. The earliest references to the druids are contained in Caesar's *Commentaries*, written about 52 B.C., in which he makes it clear that they wielded great political and judiciary power. Their power was finally broken when they were massacred in the Roman raid on Anglesey carried out by Suetonius Paulinus in A.D. 61. He cut down the druidic groves on the island and left a garrison there.

DEFEAT OF BOUDICCA

East Anglia, under their Queen Boudicca (Boadicea) revolted.

Suetonius immediately marched back from the Menai Strait with his troops, but in the meantime the Iceni, 150,000 strong, had swooped down upon the Roman centres at *Camulodunum*, *Verulam* and *Londinium*, burning and sacking the cities, and killing (if the account of Tacitus is correct) some 70,000 Romans and Romanized Britons.

The revenge of Suetonius was swift and terrible, for Boudicca and her tribesmen were utterly defeated, with even greater loss, in a pitched battle somewhere near London, and the queen in despair committed suicide.

The ravaged cities were rebuilt and fortified, and after this interlude of fire and slaughter peace reigned in southern England for over 200 years, during which time, under a succession of Roman governors, the imperial control was widened and strengthened.

ONE of the most successful of the Roman governors during this period, at least from the military point of view, was Gnaeus Julius Agricola, who held the office from A.D. 77 to A.D. 84, during which time he advanced northwards as far as the banks of the Tay in Scotland, conquering the tribes of Lowland and central Scotland. However, his gains in Scotland were not consolidated, for the Emperor Domitian decided against the idea of colonizing that land, for there was a grave risk of weakening the Roman strength by over-extending the frontiers.

During the period of Agricola's governorship he set up two chains of forts as a barrier against the warlike tribesmen of Caledonia, the most northerly running from the neighbourhood of Edinburgh to that of Glasgow and one farther south which extended from the mouth of the Tyne to Solway Firth. But about the year 116, in the reign of Trajan, there seems to have been a serious frontier raid

PUBLIUS HADRIANUS

Hadrian, Emperor of Rome from A.D. 117-138, was renowned both as soldier and administrator. He travelled extensively, visiting all the provinces of the empire and, while in Britain, caused to be built the famous Wall from Solway to Tyne which bears his name.

during which the 9th Legion, stationed at York, was destroyed while on the way to the Lowlands.

When the Emperor Hadrian began his reign in 117, the Roman Empire was at the very height of its power and he ruled over an empire which extended from the Persian Gulf to Britain and from the North Sea to the Upper Nile. Hadrian made it his business to visit all the provinces of this mighty empire, and in the year 122 he came to Britain. Of his visit he left a lasting memorial in the great Roman

SEPTIMIUS SEVERUS

Lucius Septimius Severus, Emperor of Rome A.D. 193-211, was a man of ambition and restless activity. Disliked for his severity he, nevertheless, did much to stamp out corruption in the empire and encouraged learning. He died at York on February 4th, 211.

Wall, a continuous line of fortifications with which he planned to link up the forts previously set up by Agricola between Newcastle and Carlisle. Later the Emperor Antoninus, Hadrian's adopted son, linked the northern forts in a similar manner.

Hadrian's wall, the building of which he entrusted to a general called Platorius Nepos, was a continuous patrolling system, consisting of a wall of turf rising about 20 feet above ground running right across the northern part of the country, protected in front by a deep ditch. Upon this the Emperor Severus later built a wall of stone. This wall

ROMAN BRITAIN

The remains of the mile castle at Housesteads on Hadrian's Wall. Mile castles were barracks provided for the troops manning the wall and were so named because they were the distance of a Roman mile (1,620 yds.) apart.

was patrolled along its whole length by troops lodged during their tour of duty in barracks known as mile castles, because they were that distance from one another. Each of these stations was capable of housing about 80 men.

Between each mile castle were two turrets where men could shelter and from which they could, if necessary, reach the ground. At intervals along the wall were large forts holding a permanent garrison, and there were also gates, or sally-ports, giving access to the country northward.

After the completion of Hadrian's Wall little is recorded of the happenings in Britain for some time, but while the south seems to have enjoyed a period of peace, from 180 until the end of the second century there was considerable strife in the north, where during the reign of the Emperor Commodus, invaders from Scotland pierced the wall of Antoninus and did considerable damage before being driven back by Ulpius Marcellus, a former governor of Britain whom the emperor had sent back to conduct the campaign.

In 193 Commodus was assassinated and civil war broke out in the empire. It came about in this way: The Roman

AN EMPIRE FOR SALE

Senate named Helvius Pertinax as emperor, but he was slain by the Praetorian Guards, the *corps d'élite* of the Roman army. Unbelievable as it may sound, they then offered the Roman world for sale to the highest bidder and it was sold to a wealthy senator named Didius Julianus, who was declared emperor by the Praetorians.

But this was more than the legions could stomach; the armies of Britain, of Syria and of Pannonia* refused to countenance so ignominious a bargain. Then the generals commanding the respective armies, Clodius Albinus in Britain, Pescennius Niger in Syria and Septimius Severus in Pannonia, each decided that he ought to be the successor of Pertinax.

All three were capable and experienced soldiers. Septimius Severus, being nearest, marched on Rome and disbanded the Praetorian Guard. Then, after defeating Pescennius Niger in Syria, he hastened west against Albinus,

---

* A country corresponding roughly to the territory occupied today by Austria, Hungary and part of Czechoslovakia.

Below, the remains of the West Gate at *Borcovicium*. This Roman *castella* or fort on Hadrian's Wall had four gates from each of which a street ran straight to the centre of the fort.

ROMAN BRITAIN

who had crossed from Britain into Gaul, and defeated him at Lyons.

But in order to further his ambitions Albinus had taken with him to Gaul most of the British garrison, and from the Lowlands of Scotland came the tribe of the Maeatae, and from the Highlands that of the Caledonii who seized this opportunity and destroyed the denuded fortresses of Chester and York.

And so, as soon as Severus, now Emperor, had made his position secure, he came in person to Britain, carried out a punitive expedition as far north as the Moray Firth, and restored the authority of the Romans in the north. He reconstructed Hadrian's Wall, which the Scottish invaders had destroyed in many places, building a stone wall upon the top of the older wall of turf. He died at York in February, 211.

For the next 70 years, while the Roman Empire on the Continent was undergoing a series of crises, with Gaul in open rebellion and the East setting up rival candidates for the imperial throne, Britain remained peaceful and prosperous.§

In the year 285 Diocletian (whose parents had been slaves in the house of a Roman senator) began a reign that was to be as illustrious as his birth was obscure. He divided the imperial authority, conferring that over the Western Empire upon a soldier called Maximian, on whom he bestowed the title of Augustus.

Now about this time the coast of Britain was being harassed by Frankish and Saxon pirates, and to deal with this menace the naval forces were strengthened. To take charge of the *Classis Britannica*, as this fleet was termed, Maximian appointed an officer called Carausius.

At first all went well; Carausius caught many pirate ships

---

§ *For a while Britain was nominally part of a Gallic empire, under the Emperor Postumus, until Aurelian, a soldier who had risen from the ranks to the imperial throne, by a swift series of remarkable military successes, re-established the power of Roman arms.*

The lonely land of stone and bracken which the Roman legionaries saw as they patrolled the vast rising and falling stretches of Hadrian's Wall at *Borcovicium*, a few miles from the banks of the Tyne. The wall extends for about 74 miles between Wallsend on the Tyne and Bowness on the Solway. The wall was intended to act as a defensive bulwark against raiders from the north.

laden with plunder. But instead of returning this booty to its rightful owners or handing it over to the Imperial Treasury, Carausius used it for his own benefit. It was even mooted that he had a private understanding with some of the pirates.

As soon as the affair came to light, Maximian ordered his arrest. Carausius saw that only a bold course would save his head and so he crossed to Britain and declared

ROMAN BRITAIN

This bronze head, recovered from the Thames in the vicinity of London Bridge, and now deposited in the British Museum, depicts the Emperor Hadrian. He was a patron of learning and of architecture and founded the great educational institution at Rome known as the Athenaeum, an adaptation of a similar establishment in ancient Athens, dedicated to Minerva, where poets and orators recited and philosophers and professors lectured to all interested in the liberal arts.

THE REIGN OF CARAUSIUS

himself emperor. Having won over the legions to his side he defeated such of the auxiliaries as resisted him and in the end set up an independent British Empire similar to the Gallic Empire that Postumus had ruled over (*see* footnote, page 18). This was in the year 286 or 287.

Maximian seized his possessions on the other side of the Channel and sought to attack him, but the naval power of Carausius was too great for him and his fleet was repeatedly defeated. The two Augusti,* Maximian and Diocletian, who had troubles enough to deal with in Europe, decided to accept the dictates of necessity and undertook to share the imperial power with him, and he was likewise given the title of Augustus. Carausius had set up a mint in London, and to celebrate the event coins were struck bearing the busts of the three emperors with the words *Carausius et fratres sui,* Carausius and his colleagues (literally "brothers").

Carausius reigned over Britain for seven years, apparently with great efficiency, keeping the barbarians in check and restoring the silver coinage, which for some time had ceased to exist. But in 295 he was murdered by one of his officials, Allectus, who seized power. He did not, however,

* **Augustus.** *An honorary title conferred in 27 B.C. on Octavian, the first o the Roman emperors, and assumed by succeeding emperors.*

Coins bearing the effigy of Carausius.

ROMAN BRITAIN

enjoy it for long, for in 296 Constantius Chlorus, one of the two new Caesars§ appointed by Diocletian three years previously, sailed for Britain and landed near Portsmouth. He marched towards London and on the way defeated and slew Allectus.

With the death of Allectus, Britain once again came under the central Roman government, and Diocletian, who now divided the Roman world into four portions, allotted Britain to Constantius. Various reforms, both in civil administration and with regard to the army, were instituted by Diocletian, the essence being the divorce of the military from civil power with the aim of preventing the revolt of the viceroys in the various provinces. At any rate, for more than 50 years after the downfall of Allectus Britain saw no more such revolts.

CONSTANTIUS found much to do. Like Severus at an earlier date, he rebuilt the frontier defences, which lay here and there in ruins, partly through neglect and partly as the result of repeated incursions by the barbarians. He also rebuilt the fortress of York, and erected fortifications from the Wash to the Isle of Wight along what came to be called the *Litus Saxonicum*, or Saxon Shore. In charge of these defences he appointed a senior officer with the title of "Count of the Saxon Shore," who had his headquarters at Richborough in Kent, known to the Romans as *Rutupiae*.

While conducting a successful punitive expedition against the Scottish tribes Constantius died at York (*Eboracum*) in 306, and was succeeded by his son Constantine who was proclaimed Caesar by his troops.

We have seen that Diocletian had divided the imperial authority between two *Augusti*, one ruling over the Western Empire and one over the Eastern, and each having

---

§ Caesar *was the name given, in the age of the Roman emperors, to the apparent heir to the emperor; and in the reign of Diocletian denoted a sort of junior emperor.*

RELICS OF ROMAN RULE

Above, the remains of the Praetorium, or Headquarters Building, at Housesteads (*Borcovicium*), on Hadrian's Wall, situated upon the moors some 30 miles west of Newcastle. *Below*, the ruins known as Stutfall Castle, near Lympne in Kent. This was one of the forts of the Saxon Shore (*see* p. 22) in the days when Lympne (*Lemanis*) was a naval harbour. Since Roman times the sea has receded, as at Richborough.

ROMAN BRITAIN

a *Caesar* with authority over an allotted area. But this arrangement did not endure beyond the lifetime of Diocletian himself. In the 21st year of his reign Diocletian abdicated and persuaded his colleague Maximian to do likewise; this joint abdication was followed by a period of discord and confusion, during which Constantine, a skilful and ambitious man, embarked upon the campaigns which made him master of the whole Roman World.

During the 30 years that Constantine reigned Britain enjoyed comparative peace and prosperity, although Constantine himself never visited Britain after his proclamation by the legions at York. But from the time of Constans, who succeeded Constantine in 337, trouble from invaders became more frequent. One reason may have been because the seat of government, which Constantine had transferred from Rome to the city that bears his name, Constantinople, was too far away to enable effective steps to be taken without undue delay.

FROM A.D. 350 onwards Britain had to endure a series of formidable raids which lasted for about a century by Irish, Scots and Picts along the northern frontier and west coast, and by Saxons and Franks in the south-east. Although the wall was once again repaired by the great general, Theodosius, in the reign of Valentinian, the land cleared of invaders, and both fleet and army reorganized, the rebellion of Magnus Maximus in 383 was to undo the good that Theodosius had accomplished.

In that year this Spanish officer, who had seen service under Theodosius, led a revolt against the Emperor Gratian, and was proclaimed emperor by the legions, who disliked Gratian because he had renounced the dress and manner of a Roman and accoutred himself like a Scythian warrior. After reigning for a brief space over Britain alone, Maximus claimed the empire of the West and crossed

THE END OF ROMAN RULE

to Gaul, taking with him the best troops of the British garrison, with the result that Hadrian's Wall was again overrun by northern tribes, and from then onwards it was never again restored. This depletion of the British garrisons by Maximus may be taken as the forerunner of the end of Roman rule in Britain.

For a time the Vandal general Stilicho, who became regent of the West at the death of the Emperor Theodosius, was able to drive back the invaders, but at the beginning of the fifth century he was forced, in turn, to withdraw troops from Britain to deal with the menace of Alaric, King of the Visigoths, who towards the end of the year 402 had crossed the Alps and reached Milan.

THE garrison now remaining in Britain was totally inadequate if Rome wished to retain her province, but Rome itself was in danger, and in 410 Honorius, the emperor in the West, a son of Theodosius the Great, practically wrote "finish" to the story of the Roman epoch in Britain when he refused to send any more troops to the help of the Britons in their constant wars with the Scottish, Irish and Saxon invaders and left the tribal authorities to do the best they could for themselves.

In that year, on August 24th, the Imperial city of Rome itself was sacked and pillaged by the Goths. From then on the story of Roman Britain is obscure. Whether there was a temporary reoccupation we do not know for certain, but in any case effectual Roman rule had ceased before the year 450 at the latest. For nearly 400 years Britain had been a Roman province.

★   ★   ★   ★   ★

ROMAN BRITAIN
0 10 20 30 40 50 60 Miles
Large Fortresses
Small Forts
Large Towns
Small Towns
Definite Roads
Indefinite Roads
Forests
Inchtuthill
Strageth
Ardoch
Camelon
Bodotria
Wall of Pius
Cramond
Inveresk
Carstairs
Clota
Lyne
Dere
Trimontium
Cappuck
Chew Green
Bremenium
Habitancum
Bewcastle
Blatobulgium
Hadrian's Wall
Corstopitum
South Shields
Luguvallium
(Carlisle)
Chester-le-Street
Ituna Aest
Voreda
Vinovia
Uxellodunum
Brocavum
Huntcliff
Galava
Lavatrae
Hardknott
Cataractonium
Ravenhill
Clanoventa
BRIGANTES
Scarborough
Monapia
Overborrow
Isurium
(Aldborough)
Malton
Lancaster
Eburacum (York)
(COLONIA)
Ilkley
Bremetennacum
PARISI
Cambodunum
Legiolium
Abus Aest
Coccium
Manchester
Doncaster
Warrington
Mona
Canovium
Aquae
Anavio
Lindum (Lincoln)
(COLONIA)
Segontium
Deva (Chester)
ORDOVICES
Trisantona
Metaris Aest
Caergai
CORNOVII
Derby
CORITANI
Branodunum
Viroconium
(Wroxeter)
Watling
Ratae
(Leicester)
ICENI
Gariann
Pennal
Letocetum
Venta Icenorum
(Caistor St Edmunds)
Caersws
Sabrina
Venonae
Durobrivae
Brayonium
Godmanchester
Castell Collen
Bannaventa
Ermine Street
Cambridge
Llanio
SILURES
Magnae
Lactodorum
TRINOVANTES
DEMETAE
Gaer
DOBUNI
Durocobrivae
Felixst
Maridunum
Gobannium
Glevum
(COLONIA)
(Gloucester)
Verulamium
(St Albans)
Camulodun
(Colcheste
Penydarren
Othona
Isca Silurum
(Caerleon)
Venta Silurum
Corinium
(Cirencester)
Dorchester
Londinium
Cardiff
Thamesis
Regulbi
Aquae Sulis
(Bath)
Cunetio
Durobrivae
Tana
Calleva Atrebatum
(Silchester)
Durovernum
(Canterbury)
Rutu
BELGAE
CANTIUM
Sorbiodunum
(Salisbury)
Venta Belgarum
(Winchester)
Dubra
Portus Lem
Ilchester
Clausentum
(Southampton)
Regnum
(Chichester)
Anderida
DUROTRIGES
DUMNONII
Isca
Dumnoniorum
(Exeter)
Durnovaria
Vectis
Moridunum
Gessoria
(Boulogn
Chas. E. Riddiford, del.
A
B
C
D
1
2
3
4
5
6
7

ROMAN HIGHWAYS

THE ROMANS IN BRITAIN

WHAT benefits did Britain derive, if any, from this long occupation by the Romans, is a question we may well ask. In the first place, then, we find that Britain, for the first time in history, emerges as one unified territory. Prior to the Roman Conquest Britain was composed of a great number of petty tribal states, constantly at war one with another—tribes like the Brigantes, Iceni, Catuvellauni, Silures, Belgae, Atrabates, Trinovantes, Cantii and Regni, to mention only some of them.

THE resources of the country were, in the main, unexploited. The working of metals and the use of manufactured articles were purely local. There were no roads, nor had any attempt been made to drain marshes, embank the rivers or reclaim the many vast tracts of waste land.

One of the greatest factors which helped the unification of Britain was the development of communications, and the Romans brought with them their own particular genius for constructing properly engineered highways. Thousands of miles of Roman road spread over Europe, North Africa and Asia Minor. From York to Damascus, from Tingis to Alexandria, from Cadiz to Cologne these great highways spread, and it is no exaggeration to say that a traveller in the days of the Roman Empire could have travelled faster than could William Cobbett or his contemporaries.

They were primarily military roads, constructed to enable the army to move freely. If the conquest of Britain proceeded at first by slow stages, it was because the Roman generals wanted first of all to construct roads to ensure their lines of communication. How good the road system of the Romans was is shown by the fact that so many of

ROMAN BRITAIN

Here is a portion of the old Roman road known as Erming or Ermine Street in the vicinity of Ancaster in Lincolnshire. This road went from London via Godmanchester and Castor to Lincoln and from there was continued to the River Humber, at Winteringham, by the road called High Street or Humber Street.

the main roads in use today follow almost the same course.

With no maps and no compass, and only the most primitive instruments for surveying, the Romans carried their roads exactly where they were needed for great distances, and though their comparative straightness is the characteristic which first strikes an observer, their great merit lies in the skill with which use was made of the natural features of the country, and though the general course of Roman roads in open country is straight, indeed, with hardly a deviation over long stretches, nevertheless, the Roman engineer had no compunction about making a detour to avoid unnecessary crossings of rivers or steep hills.

Roman roads varied in width according to their importance, the normal breadth of the main roads being from 20 to 24 feet. The method employed in laying the road was

THE ROAD THROUGH THE FOREST

This portion of an old Roman road, running between Lydney and Mitcheldean, lies in the Forest of Dean, Gloucestershire, and can be traced for just over ten miles. It is thought to have been built in the first or early in the second century.

to turn up the earth from two parallel ditches and between them form a bed on which the road was built up from several layers of material. On top of the soil was spread a layer of rubble stones and on top of this a bed of broken stones mixed with lime to form a concrete foundation. Then the *nucleus* was added: finely ground material mixed with lime and rammed firmly down, and on top of all were laid paving stones, four to six inches thick, which were firmly cemented. Each layer was made thinner at the edges than in the middle, thus giving the road a camber, or curve, so that the rain would run off. Their excellence is one of the reasons why the Roman roads are no longer in existence today. We can still trace their course in many places, but soon after the Roman occupation came to an end the roads were to a large extent destroyed for the sake of their materials.

The Latin word for these roads was *iter*, which has survived in our word, "itinerary," and each was given a number. But today we remember them mainly through the names given to them by the Saxons: Watling Street, Iknild Street, Erming Street and so on.

THE original Roman roads, as we have said, are gone; in fact, we can see few Roman remains in Britain, for Roman buildings, as well as Roman streets, have vanished through the centuries to provide builders and farmers with material. The Roman cities now lie buried many feet below ground level and it is only when digging for the foundations of new buildings that Roman remains come to light, as they have done recently in London.*

However, we do know what a Roman city in Britain looked like, for one of them was deliberately excavated and thoroughly investigated between 1864 and 1910. This was the Romanized capital of the old territory of the Atrabates—a town called Calleva and known today as Silchester, mid-way between Basingstoke and Reading. All that can be seen today are the remains of the walls, for

---

* See *frontispiece and illustration on page 59, and also the companion volume*, London.

ROMANIZED TOWNS

after the site had been carefully investigated the soil was replaced.

But before we describe the remains at Silchester, it will not be out of place to say a few words about the Roman towns in Britain as a whole. Urbanization, or the building of towns, was one of Rome's chief legacies to her provinces. The town was unknown in Britain before the Romans came; the nearest approach to it was the central fortress of the tribal king surrounded by the accompanying households of the nobles. There was little in the way of commerce or industry and, as wealth was almost entirely derived from the ownership of land and cattle, residence in the country was almost indispensable, and the centres of habitation in pre-Roman days were no more than clusters of rude huts.

With what astonishment, therefore, the ancient Britons must have witnessed the construction of properly planned

A Roman stile at Market Overton, in Rutland, leading from the church-yard to the site of a large Roman camp in which a cartload of Roman implements and ornaments were recovered in the stone coffin of a child.

ROMAN BRITAIN

Part of the old Roman wall at Colchester, in Essex, which lies on the site of ancient Camulodunum. It was here that the tribe of the Trinovantes were dispossessed of their lands and dwellings for the settlement of veteran Roman legionaries. The town was made a *colonia* (*see* below) in A.D. 50.

cities, one of the essential elements of Roman civilization. There were different classes of towns, and ranking first came the *coloniae*, whose inhabitants were full Roman citizens and which was, to some extent, free from interference in its affairs by the governor of the province. The first of these to be founded in Britain was Colchester, formed round a body of time-expired legionaries, who were given a grant of money and land for a farm. In addition to Colchester, three other *coloniae* are known to have been founded in England: Gloucester, Lincoln and York.

Then came the *municipium*, which, like the colony, was a community of Roman citizens. The difference between the two was, whereas, the *colonia* was formed either as a new town or by dispossessing its original inhabitants, the

A market-place in Roman London, as depicted by A. Forestier. The area of Roman *Londinium* was considerable, for on account of its incomparable geographical location, handy to the Continent whence all early trade came, it soon became an important commercial centre.

municipium was an existing native town which had citizenship conferred upon it. Each had a definite constitution, with its annually elected magistrates. The only known example of a *municipium* in Britain was Verulam (St. Albans).

Further, there was a class of tribal towns. The British tribal aristocracies very soon became Romanized, and the Roman government was always keen to stimulate the founding, in Roman style, of new towns as tribal centres. In this way the tribal units were given self-government in a manner which, though taking into account native tradition and customs, conformed to Roman usage. These towns were known as *civitates*, but though following the same constitutional pattern as the *municipium*, did not enjoy the same rights of Roman citizenship. Thus the *civitates* of the Kentish tribes was at *Durovernum Cantiacorum* (Canterbury); that of the Regni at *Noviomagus* (Chichester); the capital of the Atrabates was *Calleva* (Silchester); and that of the Iceni was *Venta Icenorum* (Caister-by-Norwich).

WE HAVE no knowledge of the exact status of London under Roman rule. It quickly became so large and of such importance that it must certainly have had magistrates and a constitution, but it was not a tribal capital. There is no evidence that it ever became a *colonia*, or even a *municipium*.

Let us return now to the ruins of Silchester, and very briefly examine the lay-out of this Romano-British town. The ground plan laid bare by the excavators reveals a city carefully planned on the rectangular chequer-board system so favoured by the Romans, to whom "four-square" was an attribute much favoured. As they were a race of soldiers they made their streets straight, so that they could the more easily be controlled in time of war. These straight, parallel streets, running north to south and east to west divided

THE STREETS OF SILCHESTER

the town into about 40 *insulae*, or islands—"blocks" they would be termed in America.

But, although the streets were planned in this symmetrical fashion, there was a certain freedom in the placing of the houses which gave a measure of variety. Not that the private houses in Silchester were very numerous, for the town never grew in the way its planners had imagined. Indeed, the population of the Romanized towns never grew as their builders hoped. Somehow, the Britons of that age did not take to town life and, as the years passed, the towns eventually decayed.

The remains of this Roman villa at *Cilurnum*, on Hadrian's Wall, show the "hypocausts" used for heating the rooms. This was a heating space below the floor, the heat of the fire being conducted through wall flues.

Although we have only the ground plan as evidence, it would seem that the houses at Silchester were similar to those inhabited by the well-to-do people throughout the Roman Empire. Some of the houses were of considerable size, one of them containing no less than 30 rooms.

The street entrance led into a passage which gave access to a large central room known as the *atrium*. Light was

ROMAN BRITAIN

Left, the *atrium*, or central room of a Roman house. The central opening in the roof had below it a tank (*impluvium*) into which rain water fell. On account of the different weather conditions prevailing in Britain, Roman houses in this country omitted the open roof.

Above, the peristyle of an ancient Roman house excavated at Pompeii. The peristyle was a sort of quadrangular garden court, colonnaded and planted with flowers and shrubs. The residential houses of the Romans in Britain usually took the form of a long corridor or veranda, with a row of rooms behind it and additional rooms in the form of a wing at one or both ends.

THE ROMAN HOUSE

admitted by a central opening in the ceiling towards which the roof sloped, so that rain water ran off and fell into a tank in the floor underneath. This tank was often turned into a decorative feature of the *atrium* by having columns and statues placed around it.

Other rooms opened off the *atrium*, including the bedrooms and the *tablinium*, or reception room, which was often used as a dining-room. This room, in turn, opened on to the *peristyle*, a garden surrounded by colonnaded walks. At the other end of the *peristyle*, opposite the *tablinium*, was the *exedra*, a hall furnished with seats, forming a counterpart to our drawing-room. Although early Roman houses were all on one floor, later, upper storeys were added to which access was provided by means of an outside staircase.

FURNITURE was simple, and couches were used rather than chairs. If the Romanized Britons followed Roman custom in everything, then they must have adopted the peculiar Roman habit of taking their meals reclining on a couch—an uncomfortable method of feeding it appears to us today!* Some of the rooms, if not all, were heated by *hypocaust*; those that were not heated in this manner may instead have been warmed by portable braziers filled with glowing charcoal, the fuel which they used for their cooking.

A word must be said about the hypocaust (an early form of central heating) because it was a typically Roman method of warming their houses and public baths.§ Hollow spaces were left under the floors and hot air from furnaces would circulate through these spaces and then up through vertical flues behind the walls. The floors of the houses

---

* The Roman reclined on his left side, leaning on his elbow, when he took his meals. The couch was made with a slight slope so that the edge came a little above the level of the table, and was known as a triclinium, a name which came by transference to mean the dining-room itself.

§ Hypocaust *is a Greek word meaning "burning below."*

37

Caerleon, or *Castra Legionis*, the camp of the 2nd Augustan Legion, was one of the three Legionary fortresses of Roman Britain. the other two being Chester and York. Outside the walls was this amphitheatre, capable of holding some 6,000 people, where gladiatorial displays and fights with wild beasts were staged.

were usually of mosaic, the best rooms in the house often boasting elaborate designs in many colours.

To return to the excavations of Silchester; in the middle of the town rose the *Basilica*, a great hall 233 feet long by 58 feet wide, with a row of Corinthian columns on each side and a semi-circular tribune at each end. It had six rooms along the side facing the street, which were probably offices, and the building seems to have combined the functions of a town hall and an exchange.

Behind the basilica was the *Forum*, or market-place, a large open square about 450 feet across, with a roofed colonnade on each side where the shops were situated. Entrance to the forum was through a monumental arched gateway at the far end. These buildings are thought by antiquarians to date from the second century A.D. There

ROMAN MOSAIC FLOORING

The Isle of Wight was conquered by the Romans soon after the Claudian invasion and Roman remains have been discovered at many different places on the island. *Below*, is the central portion of a mosaic floor of a room in a Roman villa excavated at Carisbrooke. The intricate design is made up of cubes, about half an inch square, of red, white, black, yellow and blue. The room of which this formed the flooring was about 14 ft. square.

ROMAN HIGHWAYS

Not far from Hexham, in Northumberland, can be seen these excavated remains of what was once a Roman "villa," a term denoting almost any type of rural building, but having no connection with the sort of

were also temples and a large *hospitium*, of which the modern equivalent would presumably be an hotel, adjoining which were the public baths, an essential part of every Roman town. Here would be swimming pools and what we now call "Turkish" baths. The Turkish bath habit was inherited by the Romans from the Greeks, and "when they had acquired a liking for the bath," says the author of *Roman Panorama*, "they took to it with a thoroughness and an enthusiasm unequalled in history before or since." Rome itself was said at one time to have had no less than 1,000 public baths.

Just outside the east gate of Silchester was the amphitheatre, and although the seats have long since vanished, the circular bank of earth which formed the

A NORTHUMBERLAND VILLA

suburban house to which the term is nowadays applied. Sometimes it is an elaborate house, the residence of a landlord, or maybe a farmhouse with outlying buildings such as barns and sheds.

basis of the rising tiers, as well as fragments of the walls, are still visible.

THE ROMAN VILLA

Because it played so great a part in the economy of Roman Britain it is necessary to say something here of the Roman *villa*. In the first place, it had nothing in common with the suburban residence which today bears that name. *Villa* was the Latin name for a farm or country estate, and when we speak of a Roman villa we are alluding to what was primarily an agricultural establishment, whether the home of a yeoman farmer or the country estate of a retired official. The sites of over 500 of such villas have been located in England, together with the remains of some of them, a good example being the one in Chedworth Woods, near

ROMAN BRITAIN

Cirencester (the Roman *Corinium*). The ruins were discovered, quite by accident, in 1864, since when it has been excavated and is now in the keeping of the National Trust.

This villa was built, it is thought, towards the end of the second century, and it must have belonged to a wealthy person, for no less than 32 rooms have been uncovered, whereas a more usual number of rooms is from seven to nine. Possibly it was the country house of the Prefect. It had an upper storey of wood, roofed with slate, but this, time and the ravages of the weather, destroyed. The remains that were excavated have now been covered with sheds to prevent further deterioration. These rooms were built around an open courtyard surrounded by a covered veranda off which the rooms opened. This villa had a fine set of baths, was heated by hypocaust, and the dining-room had an elaborate mosaic floor depicting the four seasons. There was a blacksmith's forge, bakery and servants' quarters, so that evidently the estate was self-supporting.

INDEED, one of the reasons why the villas continued to prosper whilst the towns decayed was because of this self-sufficiency. Its live stock would include horses, cattle, sheep and pigs and corn would be grown on the farm. In this manner it had meat, milk, cheese and bread. The wool of the sheep was hand spun and woven into cloth in the home. The large villa contained within itself all that was required in the way of resources and labour to ensure a certain standard of living.

A regards the peasantry who lived in the villages, the Roman occupation must have made comparatively little change in their lives, except that they benefited from the law and order brought into the country by the conquerors and could now live in peace. We know little of what their dwellings were like, since, not being built of stone, like

THE ROMAN VILLA AT CHEDWORTH

Here, you see part of the Roman villa in Chedworth Wood, some seven miles from Cirencester (the *Corinium* of the Romans). The ruins were accidentally discovered in 1864 by two men who were hunting rabbits. Digging to search for a ferret which they had lost in the warren, they came across a section of mosaic pavement. The ruins were subsequently excavated, and a large villa was uncovered which, from the evidence of finds made on the spot, would seem to have been occupied from a period soon after the Roman conquest until the end of the fourth century. Of its many owners, the name of one only remains, a man called Censorinus. The general plan of the house is clearly revealed and several of its tessellated floors can still be seen in the sheds built to protect them from the weather.

Most of the Roman villas which have been identified in England (about 500 in all) have a common ground-plan, in that they have a row of rooms entered from a veranda or corridor running the whole length of the front, with, in most cases, a wing jutting forward at each end. They seem to have been built in timber and plaster, with a stone foundation, and roofed with tiles or slates.

In the case of the Chedworth villa, the northern wing was apparently given over to fulling at some time after the villa was built, and a bed of fuller's earth lies nearby. It is known that by the third century A.D. the British had developed a flourishing textile industry.

The City of Bath, in Somerset, probably came under Roman rule when Suetonius conquered the south-western part of Britain during the reign of Claudius. The great baths were founded within a few years of the arrival of the legions but, strange to say, their ruins were not unearthed until 1878, and large areas as recently as 1923. The main feature of the baths was the large swimming pool seen above surrounded by a roofed colonnade. The water comes from hot underground springs.

those of the more prosperous folk, almost all trace of them eventually disappeared. They were probably no more than simple huts, with walls of wattle and daub, covered with a thatched roof.

What language these ordinary folk spoke we do not know. It probably varied in different parts of the country. In the west it was likely to have been an early form of Welsh, whereas in the south, which had been peopled by the Belgae, the common tongue may have been a Germanic dialect. As the Roman occupation extended, more and more people must have become bi-lingual, especially in the towns, since Latin was the language of all official business and of commerce. Moreover, as the Roman army of occupation

THE ROMAN ALPHABET

in Britain was a cosmopolitan one, made up of soldiers from all parts of the Roman Empire, Latin was the only tongue in which they could converse with one another; it was, if you like, a kind of Esperanto. It was not, of course, the classical Latin of a writer like Cicero, but a colloquial Latin which served as a *lingua franca* between all the races of the Empire.

That the common people of the country had some knowledge of Latin is vouched for by the inscriptions in Latin that have been found scrawled upon tiles and bricks by their makers. And not only did the Romans teach the early Britons how to read and write, but they gave us our alphabet. It is true that the Latin alphabet had been introduced into Britain before the Roman invasions, for it was used on the coins struck for British kings like Cunubeline; but it seems to have been used for no other purpose until the Romans came. This Roman alphabet, which is still the alphabet chiefly used today, reached its highest development in inscriptions incised on stone, and many such inscriptions, which were always cut in capitals, have survived to this day and can be seen in museums in the form of tombstones, building records, stamps on ingots of metal, seals and pottery and the wording on altars and the bases of statues.

Industry in Roman Britain

The effect of the Roman conquest on the industry and commerce of Britain was immediate and lasting. The Romans introduced into the country a standard of living which was incomparably higher than anything the native inhabitants had ever known. Consequently it was not long before the British aristocracy began to adopt their mode of life. This led to the importation of a great number of luxury articles into Britain by Gaulish traders.

Glassware, for instance, was common in the Roman

ROMAN BRITAIN

household, and food was served in, and rooms decorated with, the fine red glazed-ware which is often called "Samian," though none of it ever came from Samos. It derives from a red ware made at Arezzo in Italy and it spread through the empire, where it was mass-produced in potteries in Gaul

Here, we see four pots of "Castor" ware, the upper pair from Colchester and the lower from Northamptonshire. Sometimes known as "Durobrivian" ware, this pottery was decorated by hand, the ornament in relief being formed by the application of a semi-liquid "slip" (clay diluted to the consistency of thick cream). This decoration shows the survival of the Celtic tradition in Roman Britain.

and along the valley of the Rhine. We know that it was imported into Britain in large quantities, for the wreck of a ship bearing a huge consignment of second-century Samian ware, near Whitstable, was the origin of the name Pudding Pan Rock.

CRAFTS IN ROMAN BRITAIN

Also the Romans were skilled workers in glass, and considering how fragile this material is the quantity that is still in existence is remarkable. In the manufacture of iron implements, too, they were excellent craftsmen, and made and used a variety of such articles, including scythes, hatchets, crowbars, pickaxes, chisels, gouges, pocket-knives and so on.

Now the British craftsman was himself quite good at making pottery, besides being an excellent worker in metal, so it was not long before he was busy making those articles which previously his countrymen had purchased from the foreign trader. When we reach the third century, when Romanized town life was on the decline, imports also declined, and Britain came to rely more and more on its own artisans. Pewter, for instance, replaced the imported foreign silver.

WE HAVE mentioned that one of the things which may have had a bearing on the Roman conquest was the richness of mineral deposits in the land. At any rate, hardly had the Roman armies consolidated their postion in Britain than they began to work the mines, beginning with the silver-yielding lead mines of the Mendips. Silver was used

Below, Roman leaden seals found at Brough, in Westmorland. The top pair bear the mark of the 2nd Legion.

The Roman *pharos* or lighthouse on the cliffs near Dover Castle, adjoining the ancient church of St. Mary, built in part from material taken from the lighthouse. The word *pharos* is derived from the island of Pharos, off Alexandria, where Ptolemy II erected a lighthouse, the first of its kind.

TRADE IN ROMAN BRITAIN

for coinage and other purposes while there was a great demand for lead, especially for water-pipes and the linings of baths. A great quantity of this lead was exported, for Britain was the principal source of lead in the Empire, and many pigs of lead stamped with the names of Roman emperors have been found. There were lead mines also in Derbyshire, Shropshire, Flint and Yorkshire.

The Romans treated the lead by a process known as cupellation. The lead was melted in a strong current of air on a layer of bone-ash, which absorbs the lead and leaves the silver behind in the form of small pellets. The saturated bone-ash, known as *cupel* can then be treated so as to recover the lead (*see* photograph of a Roman lead working, p. 11).

Tin was obtained from Cornwall when the Romans took over the long-neglected mines, iron was worked in the Weald and the Forest of Dean, where the forests gave a good supply of charcoal, and coal was mined in the districts where it is found today.

Trade was further fostered by the development of shipping, which went hand in hand with the building of harbours, quays and lighthouses. Few examples are now left of Roman lighthouses; indeed, the only substantial remains are of the lighthouse (which the Romans called a *pharos*) on the cliff beside Dover Castle, a photograph of which you can see on the facing page.

How many things the Romans thought of as being necessary in a civilized community were neglected by succeeding generations in this country. Although to the Romans the lighthouse was a necessity if ships were to make a safe landfall, after they had departed no one troubled to build any more for centuries. Although a few beacons were lit on church towers near the coast during the Middle Ages, it was not until well into the nineteenth century that any particular attention was paid to what we now consider an elementary precaution.

ROMAN BRITAIN

It was the same with many other things. Central heating, baths and glazed windows. The windows at Silchester had glass in them, yet after the Romans had gone it was not until the thirteenth century that glass was once more to be found in English windows; and as for baths, even nineteenth-century England seemed to get along with a minimum!

Pottery

We have mentioned the Samian ware which the Romans introduced into Britain. Of Roman pottery we have a great store in our museums, whereas the textiles and the things made of wood have completely vanished. Although at the outset much of the pottery was imported, potteries soon sprang up all over the country, and pottery kilns have been found in many places. The Romans also made ceramic articles such as drain pipes and bath tubs.

The industry seems to have been divided into two branches, for in the Castor district there seems to have been a centralized industry. A large group of potteries were established permanently in one place, with large and efficient kilns, turning out a type of pottery which, though apparently having reached Britain from the Rhine district around Cologne, soon became a peculiarly British type of pottery. It is distinguished by white ornamentation in low relief on a slate-coloured ground. This ornamentation was applied by hand, whereas the Roman decoration was applied with an impressing block.

In addition to such organized potteries, in the New Forest area we find work being turned out by small independent potters who lived a nomadic life, firing their pots in small primitive kilns and hawking their wares about the country on donkey-back. They probably supplied the humbler needs of the British villagers and those who could not afford the more expensive Samian ware.

WHAT THE ROMANS WORE

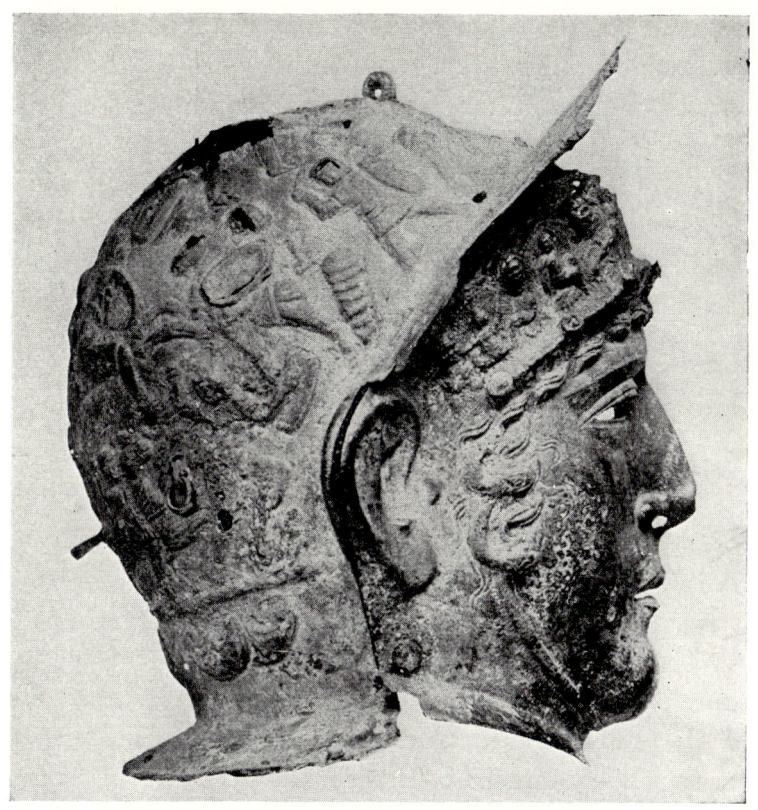

This head of a soldier wearing a bronze parade-helmet with a vizor mask was found at Ribchester, in Lancashire, and is now to be seen in the British Museum

The Garb of Roman Britain

The villager or the ordinary workman was not likely to have been much affected by what must have seemed to him the queer costumes of the Romans. He would continue to wear a short-sleeved tunic and long trousers tied around the ankles and held up by a belt, with a rough cloak fastened across the breast in inclement weather. They continued to wear their hair and their moustaches long, whereas the Roman kept his hair trimmed short and was usually clean-shaven, though he might have a beard.

The Romans, of course, brought with them their national costume, and though the number of Italian-born

ROMAN BRITAIN

Romans* in the country was probably limited to soldiers and some of the officials and magistrates, the better-off classes and the Romano-British officials would wear the Roman style of dress.

A Roman's chief outdoor garment was the *toga*, a white woollen cloak which was cut, strangely enough, in the shape of a segment of a circle. A *toga* of dark wool indicated that the wearer was in mourning, while a purple stripe extending the whole length of the straight edge indicated a magistrate or a priest. Though a majestic garment in appearance it cannot have been easy to put on and drape correctly, especially as it had no fastenings.

Under the *toga* was worn a kind of short-sleeved shirt of wool or linen known as a *tunica*, from which we derive our word "tunic." This, again, was plain if the wearer was an ordinary citizen, or bore a purple stripe from neck to waist if worn by a senator. It reached just below the knees, and was fastened at the waist with a belt. For footgear the Roman wore either sandals or slippers, or perhaps, outdoors, high leather boots laced up with leather thongs. The *calceus* or leather shoe worn in town differed in pattern and colour according to the wearer's rank.

Women wore a kind of long-sleeved tunic, called a *stola*, over an undergarment, and their outdoor mantle was a draped rectangular piece of material known as a *palla*. Hats were not worn by either sex. Instead, the Romans wore a hood or drew their outer garment over their heads.

Roman men at an early date wore their hair long and grew beards but during the time of the empire the custom was to shave or to keep the beard trimmed short. Few examples of Roman razors survive as they were made of iron and, therefore, have mostly rusted away. But there is one to be seen in the British Museum.

---

* The number of pure-blooded Romans in an Empire of such a size must have been a very small percentage of the whole. But undoubtedly the Roman soldiers who were stationed in this country intermarried with the British women; most of us in England have probably some admixture of Roman blood.

AN ARMY OF CONQUEST

Hadrian's Wall was faced by a defensive dyke which is termed a *vallum*, though strictly speaking the word should be applied to the mound which once surmounted it. A very fine example of a *vallum* is seen above, at Maiden Castle, in Dorset, though this ante-dates the Roman conquest, and was possibly constructed by Belgic tribes.

The Roman Army in Britain

The Romans took Britain by force of arms, and by the prestige of their arms they held it. The Roman garrison in Britain varied in strength from time to time, but on an average the force numbered between 30,000 and 40,000 men, most of whom were stationed in northern Britain and the Welsh hills, since the remainder of the country was peaceful.

In the Roman army the great military unit was the legion, each of which had a number and was given a silver eagle which it carried as a standard. The composition of the legion varied during the centuries, but at the time of the Roman conquest of Britain probably consisted of about 6,000 men, heavy infantry armed with javelins and swords. Each legion was divided into ten cohorts, the first of these

ROMAN BRITAIN

The barracks of the Roman station of *Cilernum*, a fortress which stood on the banks of the North Tyne, about 25 miles from Newcastle and six miles from Corbridge (the Roman *Corstopitum*). The excavated remains of the fortress cover an area of very nearly six acres and the lower parts of the walls and buildings are in good state of preservation.

numbering about 1,000 men, the others about 500. Attached to the legion was a cavalry force and bodies of auxiliary troops, foreign mercenaries who were not Roman citizens, as were the legionaries.

Each legion was under the command of a *legatus* and each cohort was led by a *praefectus*. Another officer of the Roman army familiar to most people by name, because he is mentioned in the New Testament, is the *centurion*. The centurion derived his name from the fact that he originally commanded a hundred men (later the number was 60). Though they held commissioned rank, they were more or less the counterpart of the sergeant-major of today, and were chosen from the ranks by the military tribunes, who were the chief officers of the legion after the *legatus*. The centurions' badge of office was a stick (*vitis*), which they

THE ROMAN LEGIONS

often used to good effect on the backs of recalcitrant soldiers. Like the sergeant-major of a modern army they often had hard things said about them, and like the sergeant-major, also, they were the backbone of the army.

Each legionary wore a leather tunic reinforced with metal plates, called a *lorica*, a bronze helmet (*cassis*), and carried a rectangular shield about 4 feet long by 2½ feet wide. His javelin (*pilum*) had a pointed iron head fixed on a wooden shaft, and the short sword (*gladius*) was pointed and double-edged, so that it could be used either for thrusting or cutting. The auxiliaries wore a leather jerkin without armour reinforcement, an oval shield, and a longer sword, which was known as a *spatha*.

The *velites* of the early days of the Roman army were light troops, or skirmishers, and their sole protection was a plain helmet and a circular shield. Their weapons were a sword and a short javelin which they hurled at the enemy. The legionaries proper were heavy infantry, and when on the march " heavy " was the right word, for in addition to the weight of his breastplate, stout shield and weapons, the legionary was weighed down with rations for two or three weeks' campaigning, a cooking pot, together with stakes and tools of various kinds. Fully loaded in this fashion, he was described as *impeditus*, and impeded he must have been with so much equipment.

But the Roman soldier's rigorous training endowed him with great powers of endurance, and he was normally expected to cover at least 20 miles a day at the regulation rate of four miles an hour.

Infantry formed the bulk of the Roman army, which looked to its allies, or *socii*, to provide the cavalry, and it was not until the last days of the Empire that the Romans themselves brought into being a large force of cavalry to deal with the hordes of barbarian horsemen who were attacking its frontiers.

ROMAN BRITAIN

Apart from their value as cavalry, the auxiliaries played at first a very minor part in the composition of the Roman army, but ultimately they became fully as important as the legions themselves. The rank and file of the auxiliaries (their chief officers were Roman) were levied from those who were in the early days subjects but not citizens of Rome. On discharge they were rewarded with the Roman franchise.

As might be expected in an army of such prowess and prestige, discipline was exceedingly strict, with penalties for offences which ranged from flogging or loss of pay to death. But in no army was greater honour bestowed for distinguished conduct in the field.

Among the legions which are known to have been stationed in Britain are the 2nd Legion (*Augusta*), which was recruited from tribes along the Rhine and after the conquest was stationed first at Gloucester and later at Caerleon; the 9th Legion (*Hispana*) recruited in Spain, and stationed at Leicester, Lincoln and York; the 6th Legion, which replaced the 9th in the second century after the latter had been badly cut up while on their way to Scotland; the 14th Legion, known to have been stationed at Wroxeter and Chester; and the 20th Legion, which replaced the 14th Legion at Chester after A.D. 68, and that town remained its headquarters. It was used for garrison duty in many parts of Britain especially in defending Hadrian's Wall.

The Religion of the Romans

Although the Roman occupation of Britain lasted for so long, it did not profoundly affect religion in Britain, and though the Romans dealt drastically with the Druids, whom they considered a source of danger to the state, they made no attempt to interfere with the various local pagan cults of the British tribes. As long as they paid respect to the

RELIGIOUS LIFE

altar of the Emperor they could profess what other religion they chose.

The primitive Roman religion was animism, the attribution of supernatural qualities to natural phenomena and inanimate objects. To the early Roman the *numen*, or spirit, was especially localized in trees, rocks and streams; such spirits had to be propitiated by offerings and ritual.

This primitive religion underwent considerable modification as a result of the influence of Greek thought, and the old Roman *numina* gradually became identified with the Greek gods, and endowed with similar myths, Jupiter becoming identified with Zeus, and so on.

An aerial view of the Roman fort at Richborough. In Roman times it was accessible by sea, but in the intervening centuries the sea has receded, leaving a wide expanse of flat pasture land. An enormous quantity of Roman relics have been found on this site, including the cross-shaped construction, visible above, some 86 feet long and rising about 5 feet above the platform on which it stands. Richly carved fragments of white marble were dug up all around it.

Aerofilms Ltd.

ROMAN BRITAIN

MUCH of the Roman religion centred round the home, for the home was the centre of Roman life. The *Lares* were the spirits of ancestors and each home had its special *Lars familiaris*, who was worshipped at all events intimately connected with family life, such as birth, death and marriage. The *Penates* were the gods of the household stores, while *Vesta* was the spirit of the hearth. This sense of a divine presence intimately connected with all family affairs, calling as it did for the observance of proper relations (*pietas*, from which our word "piety" derives) with gods, family, and by extension, the State, strengthened that family tie which formed the basis of Roman society.

The State being, in Roman eyes, the supreme family, had its own hearth and its own *Lares* and *Penates,* and we know that the Vestal Virgins kept burning the hearth fire of the State throughout Roman history. This led eventually to emperor-worship, the Emperor being looked upon as the father of his people. One of the contributory reasons of the revolt of Queen Boudicca and the Iceni in A.D. 61 was resentment at the taxes required for the maintenance of the Temple of Claudius in the new Roman city of Camulodunum.

Later on in Roman history new religious influences came from the East, and one of these found great favour with the army. This was the cult of the Persian god of light, Mithras, a cult which the Roman army carried with it to the remotest parts of the Empire. Remains of a temple of Mithras were discovered long ago at Housesteads in Northumberland, and quite recently another has been found during building operations in the heart of London (*see* photograph on facing page and frontispiece).

About A.D. 312 occurred an event of singular importance in Roman history, for the Emperor Constantine was converted to Christianity. As a consequence it became first a tolerated religion in the Empire and, following the defeat

THE CULT OF MITHRAS

of Licinius in 324, an event which gave Constantine sole power over the Roman world, it became its State religion.

Yet in A.D. 314 there was already an organized Christian Church in Britain, for at the Synod of Arles held in that year three British bishops, as well as a priest and a deacon, were present. Other references in literature also tend to confirm the supposition that an organized Christian church existed in Britain at the very beginning of the fourth century. How, then, did Christianity come to Britain?

Legends, as usual, are plentiful. St. Peter is said to have been in Britain at the time of the Iceni rising. St. Paul

During the course of excavations on a site near Walbrook, in the City of London, there came to light in September, 1954, a *Mithraeum* or temple devoted to the cult of Mithras. This was a mystic cult, with secret rites, of Persian origin, which was widespread among the Roman soldiery during the second and third centuries A.D. *Above*, are seen front-face and profile views of the head of Mithras dug up during the excavations. A Mithraic shrine had been previously discovered in 1950 at Carrawburgh, on the Roman Wall.

ROMAN BRITAIN

himself is stated to have preached the Gospel in this country. There is also the story of St. Joseph of Aramathea who, about A.D. 63, brought the Holy Grail and the spear with which Longinus wounded the Saviour on the Cross to Britain, and founded the abbey of Glastonbury.

We know not. Christianity was certainly brought to this country while it was under Roman rule. The Roman brought the cult of Mithras to our shores. May he not have brought Christianity also? For though in general, the Roman soldier seems to have been but little influenced by Christianity we know that a great many kinds of foreign worship were brought over by the Romans and their auxiliaries, from Teutonic cults to that of the Asiatic Cybele. There were Christian churches at Silchester during the time of the Romans. It is quite possible that many others lie buried and hidden, perhaps for ever, from the eyes of men.

★ ★ ★ ★ ★

THE AFTERMATH

Of the state of affairs which existed in Britain after the departure of the Romans we have no very clear idea in the absence of written records.

It was about the year 401 when Stilicho had to withdraw troops from Britain for his war against the Goths, and although Alaric, the chief of the Visigoths, was halted at the battle of Pollentia, the danger still existed, and it is unlikely that any of the British troops of Stilicho were sent back.

By 410 there were still a garrison of sorts in the island, but they were leaderless. Since 406 the army left in Britain had itself set up a series of local emperors: first Marcus, then Gratian, and lastly a certain Constantine, but the first

THE AFTERMATH

two were short-lived and Constantius, acknowledged as emperor of Britain by Honorius, crossed over to Gaul.

The Britons thereupon expelled Constantine's governors, but although left by the Roman emperor to defend herself as best she could, Britain still kept her allegiance and affirmed her loyalty to Honorius.

But Honorius at the time was powerless to help them, for that able warrior Stilicho had been executed in 408 and now Alaric was again marching on Rome. So Honorius instructed the tribal authorities in Britain to carry on the work of government both in the military sphere and in the field of civil administration until such time as he could appoint new governors and military leaders.

This meant that the law known as *Lex Julia Majestatis* had to be relaxed, for under this law, during the Roman occupation, none but the Roman soldiers were allowed to carry arms. Obviously if the Romanized Britons were to protect themselves in the absence of adequate Roman forces, that law had to go by the board.

What happened after 410 is largely surmise. It was once thought that Britain ceased to be a part of the Roman empire from that date, but some authorities now hold that there was a final phase of Roman government which began about 417 and lasted for roughly a decade.

It is probable that both parties considered that the former connection would, in time, be restored, for Britain still belonged nominally to the Roman empire. The Romans had not abandoned their claim to Britain, nor did Britain deliberately refuse her allegiance. But soon all hope of further co-operation was abandoned and by 430 government had devolved upon the tribal communities.

Unfortunately the richness of the country, developed by the Romans during their four centuries of occupation made Britain the coveted prey of aggressors. From an early period the Saxon raiders had never ceased to make sporadic

ROMAN BRITAIN

attacks upon the British coast and only the prestige of Roman arms had kept them from making large-scale forays.

Once the Roman garrisons had departed it was not long before Saxons from south and east and Picts, Scots and other races from north and west, began to ravage the land. The Britons might have resisted the barbarians successfully had they been able to rely on experienced leaders. But for nearly 400 years the Romano-Britains had beeen trained to obey, and as a result of power having for so long been retained by the officials and generals of the Roman government, they had lost all initiative.

There was no longer any central authority and the administration of the whole country gradually collapsed. Law and order, terms synonymous with Roman rule, soon ceased to be. The Dark Ages had begun, and it took Britain centuries to recover her grip on civilization. The ease with which it can be lost should give us much to think about in these troubled times.

INDEX

ILLUSTRATIONS in bold type thus **42**

Agricola, 8, 13, 15
Alaric, 25, 61
Allectus, 21, 22
Alphabet, Roman, 45
Anglesey, 11
Antoninus, 15
Antoninus, Wall of, 16
Army, The Roman, 53, 54, 55, 56
Atrium, 35, **36**, 37
Aurelian, 18

Basilica, 38
Bath, the Roman bath at, **44**
Belgae, 7
Boadicea, *see* Boudicca
Borcovicium, **17**, **19**, **23**
Boudicca, Queen, 13, 58
Boulogne, 6
Brigantes, 10

Caerleon, Amphitheatre at, **38**
Caesar, G. Julius, 3, 4, **5**, 6, 7, 8
Caister-by-Norwich, 34
Calceus, 52
Caledonia, 13
Caledonii, 18
Caligula, 9
Calleva, *see* Silchester
Camulodonum, 10, 11, 13
Canterbury, 7, 34
Caractacus, 10
Caradoc, *see* Caractacus
Carausius, 18, 19, 21
———, Coins of, **21**
Cartismandua, Queen, 10
Cassis, 55
Cassivellaunus, 3, 7, 8
Castor, 50
Castor ware, **46**
Catuvellauni, 3
Centurion, 54, 55
Chedworth Woods, 41
Chester, 18
Chichester, 34
Cilurnum, **35**, **54**
Cirencester, 41
Civitates, 34

Classis Britannica, 18
Claudius, 8, 9, 10
Clodius Albinus, 17, 18
Colchester, 32
Colchester, Roman Wall, **32**
Coloniae, 32
Commius, 3, 4, 8
Commodus, 16
Constans, 24
Constantine, 22, 24, 59, 60
Constantius Chlorus, 22
Corinium, *see* Cirencester
Cunobeline, 10
Cymbeline, *see* Cunobeline

Didius Julianus, 17
Dio Cassius, 9
Diocletian, 18, 21, 22, 24
Domitian, 13
Dover, 3
Druids, 11, **12**

Eboracum, *see* York
Erming Street, **28**, 30
Exedra, 37

Forest of Dean, **29**, 49
Forum, 38

Garb, Roman, 51, 52
Gladius, 55
Gloucester, 32
Gratian, 24

Hadrian, 14, **14**, 20
Hadrian's Wall, 15, **16**, **17**, 18, **19**, **23**, 25, **35**
Hayling Island, 9
Helvius Pertinax, 17
Honorius, 25, 61
Hospitium, 38
Housesteads, **16**, 59
Hypocaust, **35**, 37, **42**

Iceni, 11, 13, 34
Iknild Street, 30
Insulae, 35
Iter, 30

63

INDEX

(continued)

LARES AND PENATES, 58
Lead mines, 10, **11**, 47, 49
Legatus, 54
Legion, 2nd, 9, 10, 56
——, 8th, 9
——, 9th, 9, 10, 14, 56
——, 10th, 4
——, 14th, 9, 56
——, 20th, 9, 56
Licinius, 60
Lighthouse, Dover, **48**, 49
Lincoln, 32
Litus Saxonicum, 22
Londinium, 13, **33**, 34
Lorica, 55

MAEATAE, 18
Magnus Maximus, 24, 25
Maximian, 18, 21
Medway, River, 10
Mithras, 59, **59**
Moray Firth, 18
Mosaic flooring, 37, **39**, 42
Municipium, 32, 34

OSTORIUS SCAPULA, 10

PALLA, 52
Pannonia, 17
Parade helmet, bronze, **51**
Peristyle, **36**, 37
Pescennius Niger, 17
Pilum, 55
Platorius Nepos, 15
Plautus, Aulus, 9, 11
Postumus, 18, 21
Pottery, 46, 47, 50
Praefectus, 54,
Praetorian Guards, 17

RELIGION, 57-60
Richborough, **6, 7**, 9, 22, 57
Roads, Roman, 10, 27, **28, 29**, 30
Roman pottery, 11

Rutupiae, *see* Richborough

SAMIAN WARE, 50
Sandwich, 6
Saxon Shore, 22
Seals, leaden, **47**
Severus, Septimius, 15, **15**, 1̇
  18, 22
Silchester, 30, 31, 34, 35
Silures, 10, 11
Solway Firth, 13
Spatha, 55
St. Joseph of Aramathea, 60
St. Paul, 60
Stile, A Roman, **31**
Stilicho, 25, 61
Stola, 52
Strabo, 8
Stutfall Castle, **23**
Suetonius Paulinus, 11, 13

TABLINIUM, 37
Tacitus, 8, 9, 13
Thames, River, 10
Theodosius, 24, 25
Toga, 52
Togodumnus, 10
Trajan, 14
Tunica, 52
Tyne, River, 13

ULPIUS MARCELLUS, 16

VALENTINIAN, 24
Vallum, **53**
Velites, 55
Verulam, 4, 13, 34
Vesta, 58
Villa, Roman, **40**, 41, **43**

WALMER, 4
Watling Street, 30

YORK, 18, 22, 32

―――――― ACKNOWLEDGMENT ――――――

Illustrations on pages 5, 14, 15 and 36 (both) are reproduced by permission of the Mansell Collection; 6, 7, 11, 12, 16, 17, 19, 23 (both), 28, 29, 31, 32, 33, 35, 38, 40, 43, 53 and 54, Picture Post Library; 20, 46 and 51, British Museum; 44, The Roman Baths Museum, Bath; 57, Aerofilms Ltd.; 59, L.E.A. The Map on page 26 is reproduced by permission of the Clarendon Press.